AVENGERS

Thor banishes his evil brother Loki to the Island of the Trolls.

Loki sends an evil troll to Earth to cause mischief.

The troll destroys a bridge!

Scientist Bruce Banner sees trouble at the bridge . . .

. . . and soon the Hulk comes to the rescue!

Dalmatian Press

Iron Man answers the call for help!

Ant Man and Wasp fly into action!

Captain America to the rescue!

Captain America, Iron Man, Ant Man, and Wasp think
Hulk was the one who smashed the bridge.

Thor's hammer stops the fight!

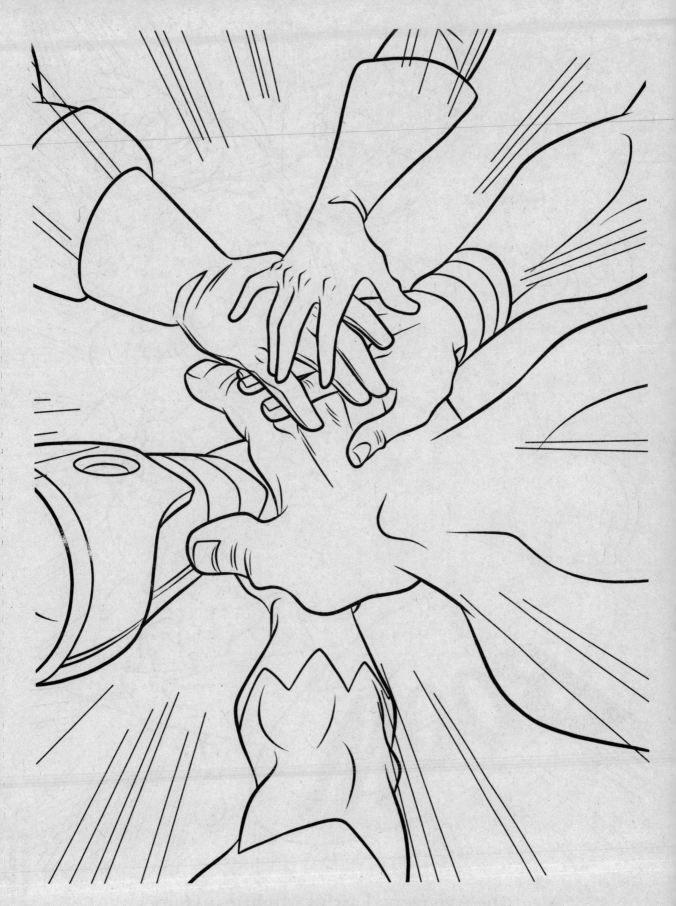

The heroes decide to join forces!

Meet the Avengers: Earth's Mightiest Heroes!

The Invincible Iron Man!

The Mighty Thor!

The Incredible Hulk!

Ant Man and Wasp!

Captain America!

Thor brings his new teammates to Asgard to
help him stop Loki.

The Avengers arrive on the Island of the Trolls.

Hulk punches the ground, scattering the trolls
that are attacking Iron Man!

Captain America battles trolls!

Wasp and the Hulk battle against a ferocious troll!

Ant Man is tiny, but he packs a big punch!

Thor defeats Loki with some help from Wasp and Ant Man!

Jarvis welcomes everyone to the Avengers Mansion.

Even the Avengers need to relax.

Tony Stark is tinkering in his lab when the
Avengers' alarm sounds!

Baron Zemo is up to no good! The streets of New York
are covered in his sticky glue!

Cap calls the team together with the Avengers' battle cry!

Dalmatian Press

Tony Stark quickly dons his armor.

The Mighty Thor is ready for action!

Ant Man and Wasp streak to Cap's side!

Scientist Bruce Banner transforms into the Incredible Hulk!

The Avengers assemble!

With the city immobilized, Baron Zemo's crimebots run wild!

The Avengers arrive, and the crimebots attack!

Iron Man blasts a crimebot!

When the Avengers are in big trouble, Ant Man
can become Giant Man!

Hulk smashes the crowd of crimebots!

Thor thwarts an attack by Baron Zemo's glue gun!

Cap distracts the Alpha-Bot while Wasp tries to disable it!

Wasp removes the battery from the Alpha-Bot and the
crimebots are disabled!

Baron Zemo flees!

Captain America throws his mighty shield!

Cap's shield causes a sticky problem for Baron Zemo!

Hulk takes out the trash!

Thor and Cap set things straight.

The Avengers return home for some well-deserved rest.

Games and Activites with the
AVENGERS!

Spot the fake! Five of these pictures show the real Hulk. One is a troll in disguise! Circle your answer.

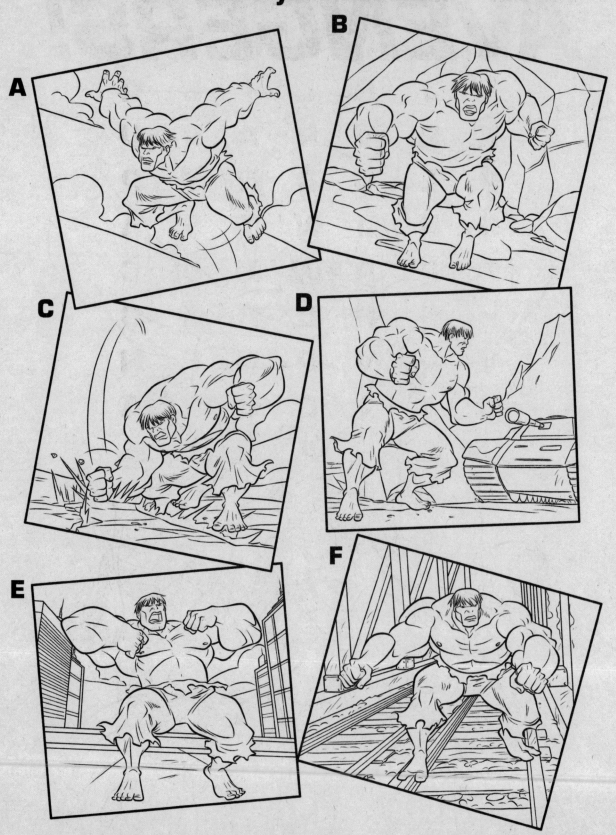

A

B

C

D

E

F

Search up, down, forward, backward, and diagonally to find all the names.

IRON MAN　　**WASP**　　**ANT MAN**　　**CAP**　　**HULK**　　**THOR**

```
K  L  U  H  M  C  Y
I  J  Q  L  I  B  R
K  K  R  V  R  A  R  U
P  P  L  O  C  N  Y  P
S  S  H  J  N  T  S  A
T  T  P  A  W  M  D  C
H  H  S  R  C  A  A  O
V  V  P  V  P  N  F  N
C  C  J  I  O  G  R  A
W  W  A  S  P  O  T  E
```

Help Tony Stark pick the right suit of armor. Circle your answer.

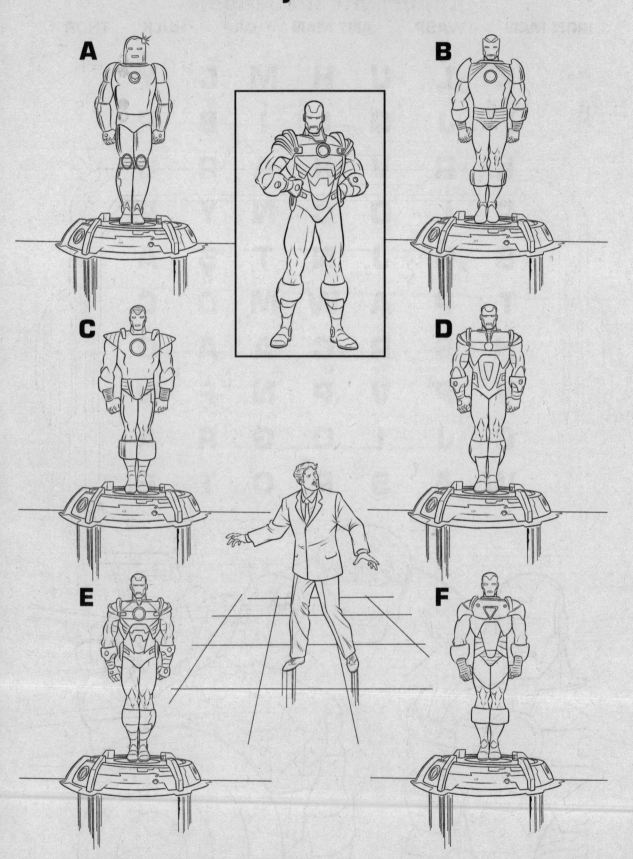

A

B

C

D

E

F

Help Tony Stark decode this important message.

Answer: Bridge Smashed! Help!

Using the grid as a guide, draw the Incredible Hulk.

Help Hulk hold up a damaged bridge by connecting the dots.

Help the Avengers find their way through Asgard to the ship.

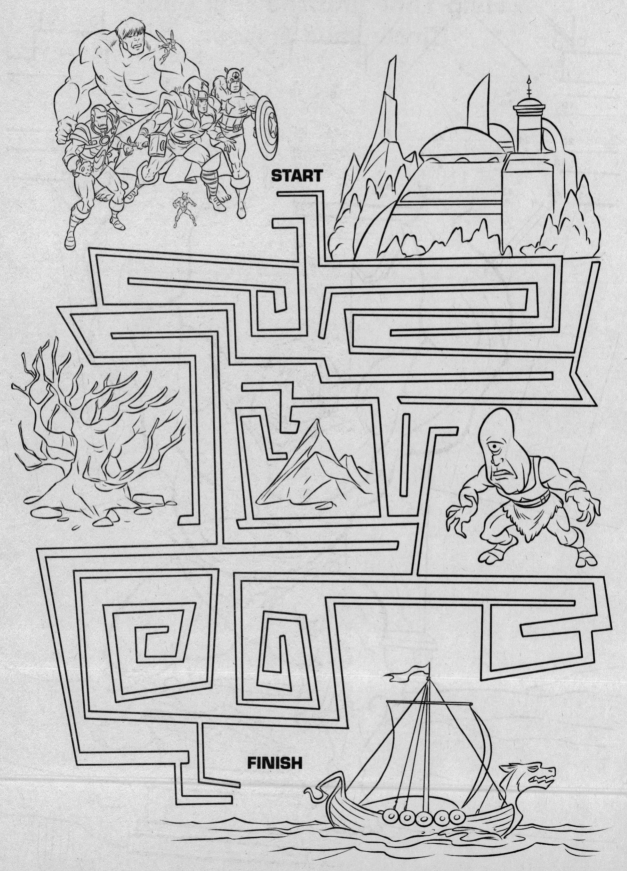

START

FINISH

Friend or foe? Loki has transformed five trolls into copies of Captain America.
Help Thor find the real Cap!
Circle your answer.

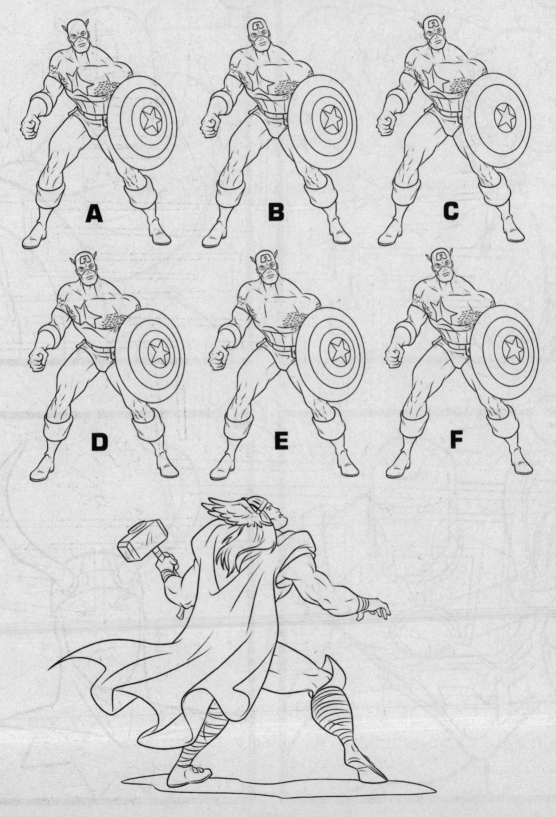

A   B   C

D   E   F

Answer: F

Who doesn't belong in this group of Avengers?

A

B

C

D

Answer: D

Help the Avengers make their way back to Earth on the Rainbow Bridge.

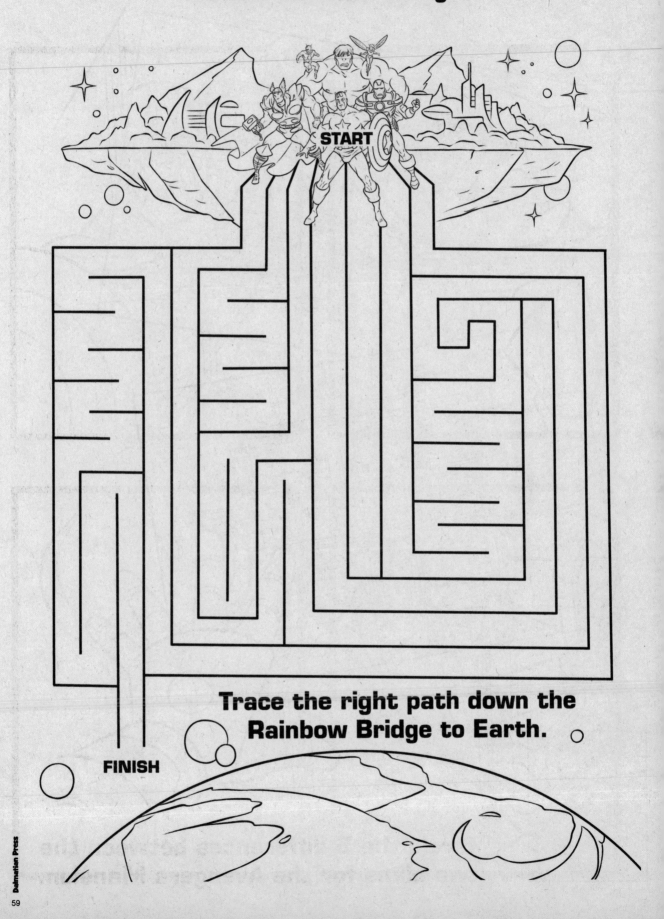

START

Trace the right path down the Rainbow Bridge to Earth.

FINISH

Tony Stark has bought a new headquarters for the World's Mightiest Heroes.

Circle the 5 differences between the two plans for the Avengers Mansion.

Answer:

The Avengers Mansion is a mess!
Help Jarvis find Cap's shield!

Answer:

Dalmatian Press

Tony Stark needs to put the pictures of the Avengers into the right folders. Draw a line between each hero's picture and the folder with his or her real name.

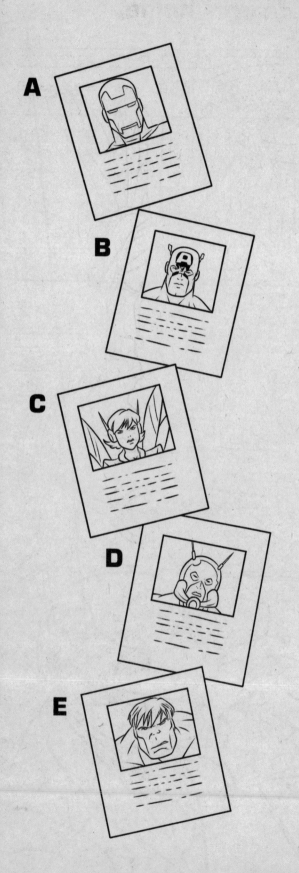

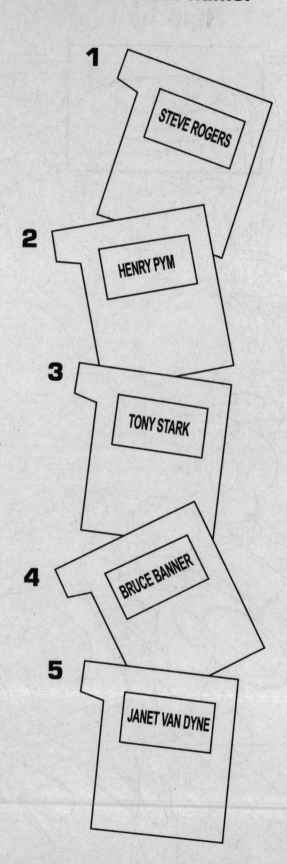

A

B

C

D

E

1 STEVE ROGERS

2 HENRY PYM

3 TONY STARK

4 BRUCE BANNER

5 JANET VAN DYNE

Ant Man is lost in the grass outside the Avengers Mansion.
Help him find the safe way home.

START

FINISH

Help Captain America decode the message from S.H.I.E.L.D.!

Using the grid as a guide, draw Iron Man.

Dalmatian Press

Help Iron Man find Ant Man and Wasp in the lab.

How many words can you make using the letters in:

AVENGERS
ASSEMBLE

_____   _____

_____   _____

_____   _____

_____   _____

_____   _____

_____   _____

_____   _____

_____   _____

Hint:
Letters may be
used more
than once.

Dalmatian Press

Possible Answers: an, age, am, able, are, be, been, beg, bag, ban, gave, rave, save, rage, nag, leg, lava, see, bee, men, ear, rang

START

Help Captain America find the sinister Baron Zemo!

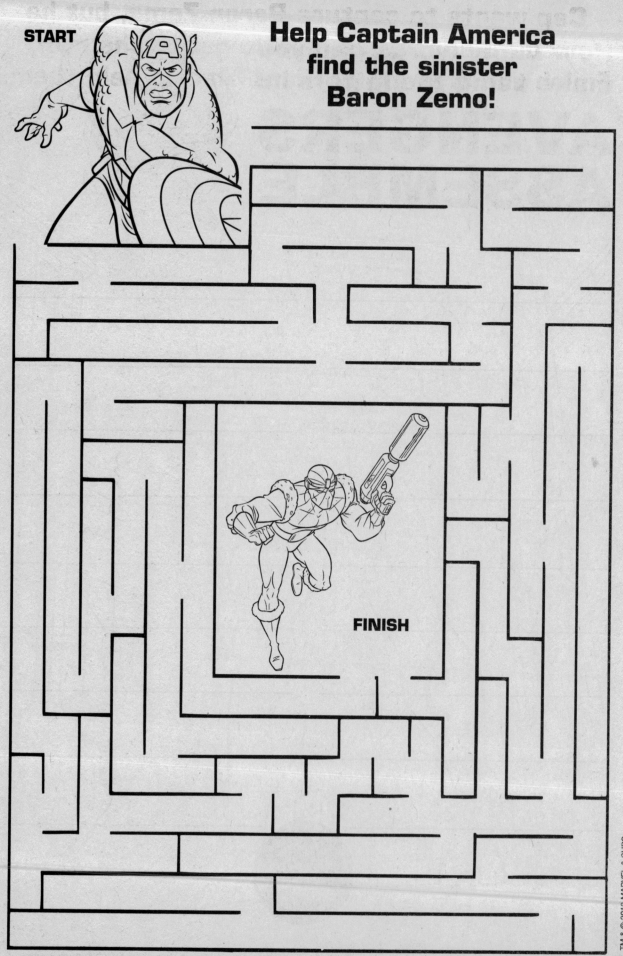

FINISH

START

Cap wants to capture Baron Zemo, but he needs Giant Man's help to get to the roof. Finish the drawing of Giant Man to help them.

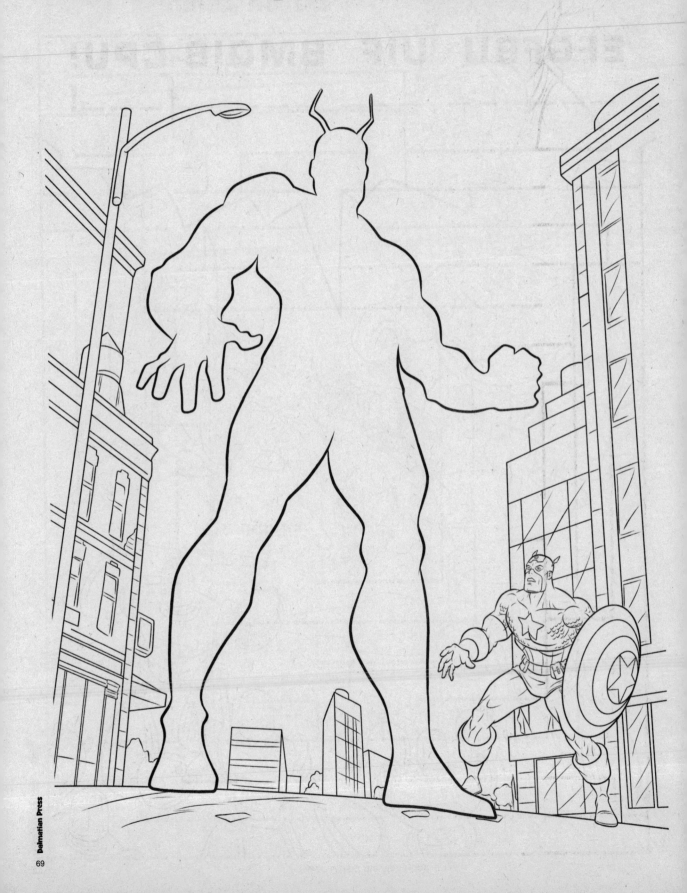

**Iron Man knows how to defeat the crimebots.
Replace each letter with the letter that comes before
it in the alphabet to find out what he tells the Avengers.**

EFGFBU UIF BMQIB-CPU!
_ _ _ _ _ _   _ _ _   _ _ _ _ _ - _ _ _ !

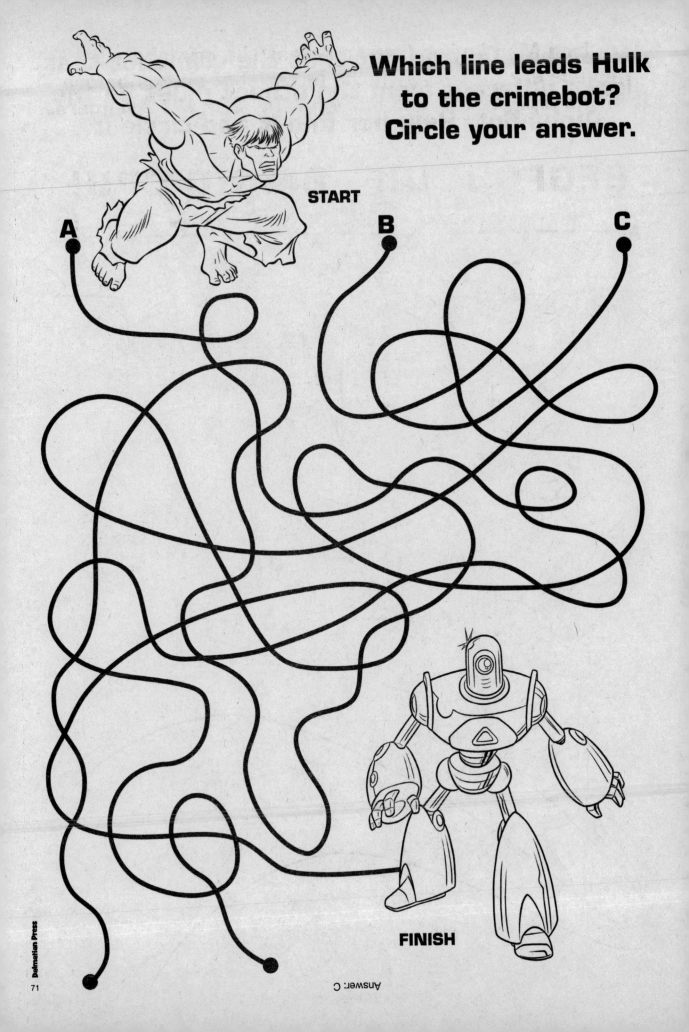

Which line leads Hulk to the crimebot? Circle your answer.

START

A   B   C

FINISH

Answer: C

Dalmatian Press

Wasp has figured out that the crimebot that looks different from the others must be the Alpha-Bot. Help her find it and circle it.

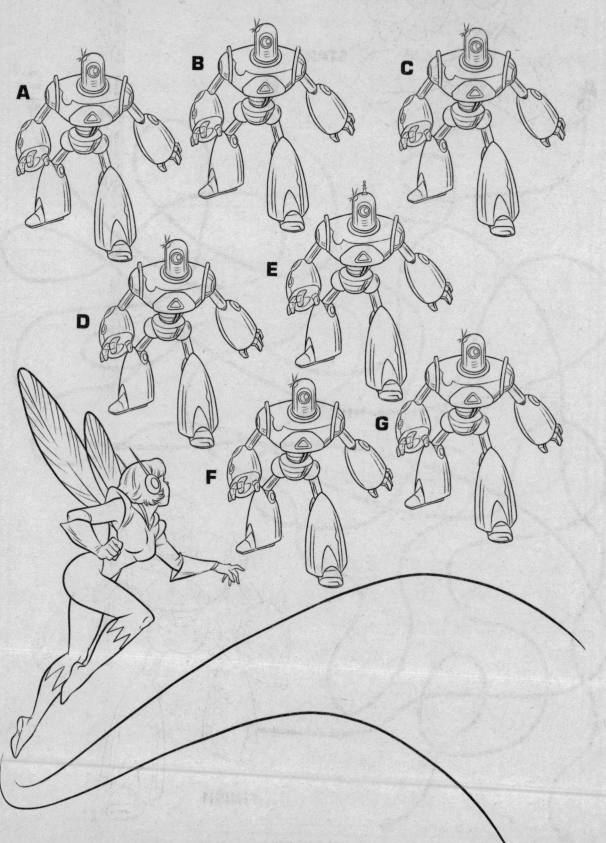

Everyone has a secret number. Can you figure out which one?

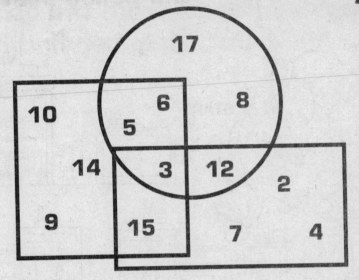

10 17 6 8
5
14 3 12 2
9 15 7 4

Thor's number is inside the rectangle. It is less than 5. It is odd. What's his number?

Cap's number is inside the circle. It is also inside the square. It is even. What's his number?

Ant Man's number is greater than 8. It is odd. It is inside the rectangle. What's his number?

Hulk's number is outside the circle. It is also outside the rectangle. It is a multiple of 3. What's his number?

Answers: Thor-3, Cap-6, Ant Man-15, Hulk-9

Help Giant Man carry Baron Zemo to the police station.

START

FINISH

POLICE

Iron Man has gotten a coded message from S.H.I.E.L.D.!
Decode it to find out what it says.

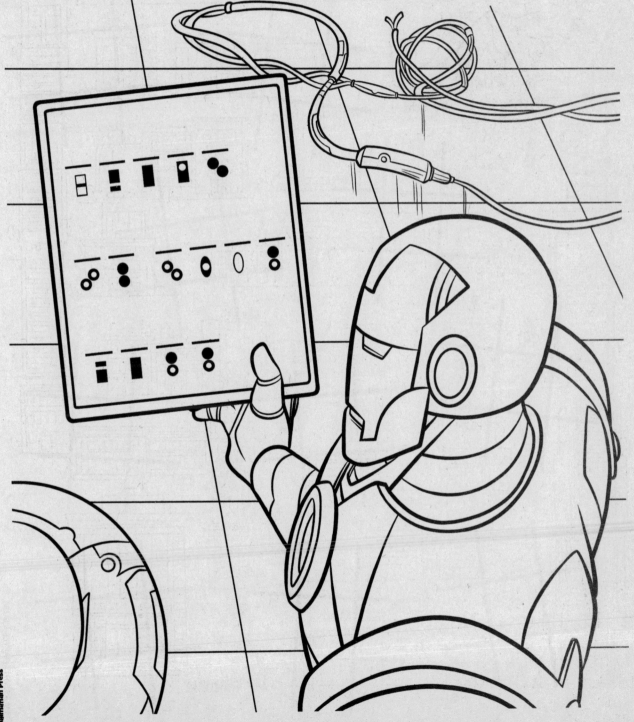

Answer: Clean Up This Mess

Dalmatian Press

Hulk is ready for a battle of TIC-TAC-TOE!

Help Giant Man shrink and find his way through the maze to team up with Wasp!

START

FINISH

Dalmatian Press

Thor has lost his helmet, hammer, and cape. Draw new armor for him.

Bruce Banner lost some important things the last time he transformed. Help him find them.

Answer:

Player #1 draws a line to connect two dots. (You can draw up and down, or across, but not diagonally.) Then Player #2 connects two dots. When a player connects two dots and completes a square, he puts his initial inside the square and takes another turn. When all the dots are connected, the game is over. Each initialed square is one point. Squares with Iron Man are worth two points. The player with the most points wins!

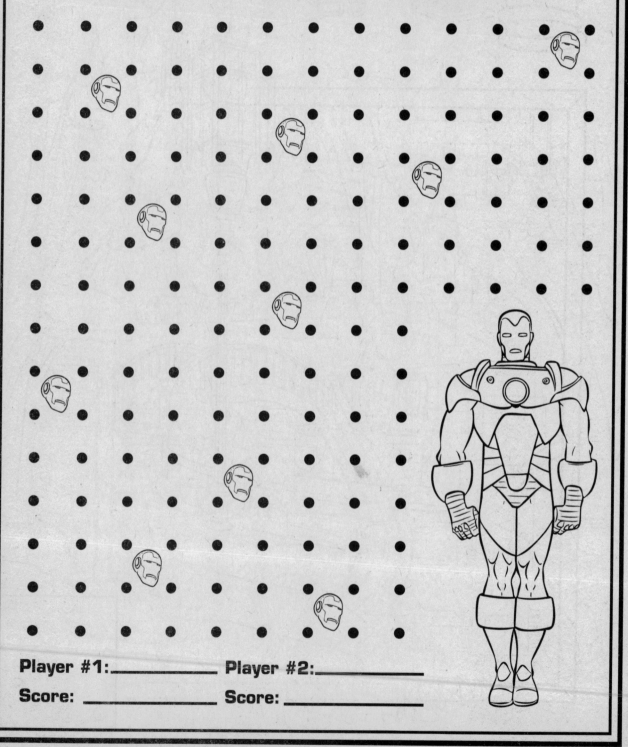

Player #1:_____ Player #2:_____

Score: _____ Score: _____

Wasp needs to remove the battery from the Alpha-Bot's circuit board.
Help her find it.

Answer:

Captain America is sending a message. Count every third shield to spell it out.

L H S P J

T R V A B C n U I

D W O F P E O Y C

R I P F T S R O A

E B D E Y K D n E

O n C M J H

___ ___ ___ ___ ___ ___ ___ ___ ___ ___ ___ ___ ___ ___ ___!

Help Jarvis match the items on the floor to the proper hero's costume. Draw a line from each item to the picture of its owner.

Answers: 1-B, 2-C, 3-D, 4-A

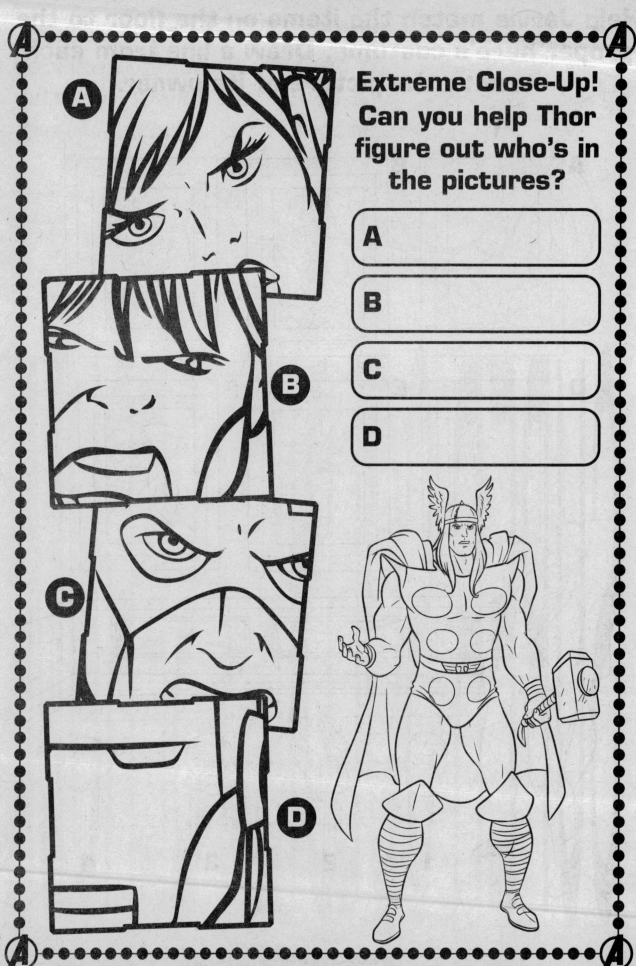

**Extreme Close-Up!
Can you help Thor
figure out who's in
the pictures?**

A

B

C

D

What caused Steve Rogers to become Captain America? To read the answer, lift the bottom of the page toward your face and tilt the page top-downward.

SUPER SOLDIER SERUM

Answer: Super Soldier Serum

Help Thor and Captain America figure out where to hang the signs. Draw a line from each sign to the store it matches.

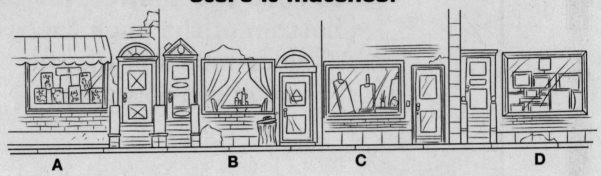

KIRBY ART SUPPLY

Which puzzle piece completes the picture?

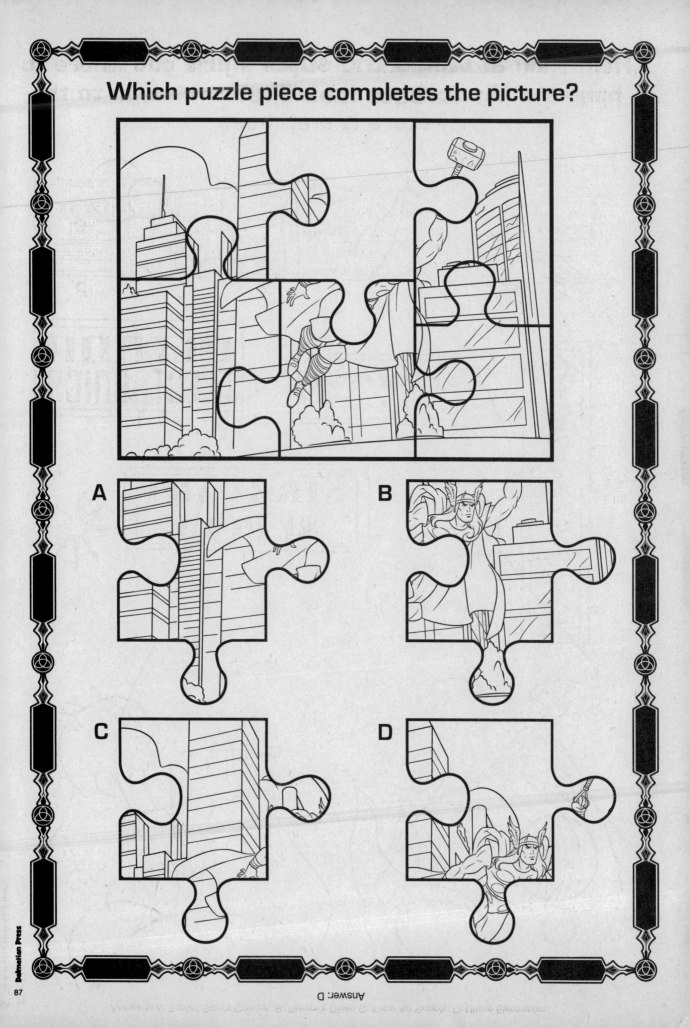

A

B

C

D

Answer: D

What would the super hero you create look like?

Can you unscramble the names and match the names and faces?

A

1. NATPAIC RMEAACI

_____

B

2. BNEREDIILC KLUH

_____

C

3. NROI NMA

_____

D

4. HTRO

_____

Answers: 1. Captain America - B, 2. Incredible Hulk - C, 3. Iron Man - D, 4. Thor - A

Write down every fourth letter in the spiral to reveal a message from Captain America.

__ __ __ __ __ __ __

__ __ __ __

__ __ __ __ __ !

Look up, down, across, and diagonally for these words.

DR PYM	STEVE ROGERS	INCREDIBLE
SCIENTIST	SOLDIER	TONY STARK
HELMET	SHIELD	GENIUS
WEAPON	BRUCE BANNER	ARMOR

R H I E L S O L D I E R

E D N M P T Y T E U S I

N O C P H A G A G R C L

N Z R C Y C N E E Y O T

A T E D S V C G N S S O

B E D E H G O T M I A N

E M I P I R E Y T R U Y

C L B I E M P N R O D S

U E L V L R E P Z M A T

R H E T D I L T G R N A

B T O I C N T V G A T R

S T B S V W E A P O N K

Dalmatian Press

Help Tony Stark suit up as Iron Man by filling in the boxes with words that rhyme with

MAN

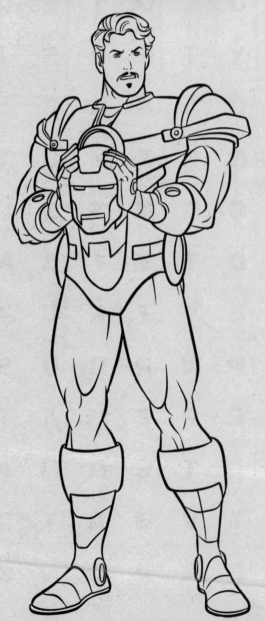

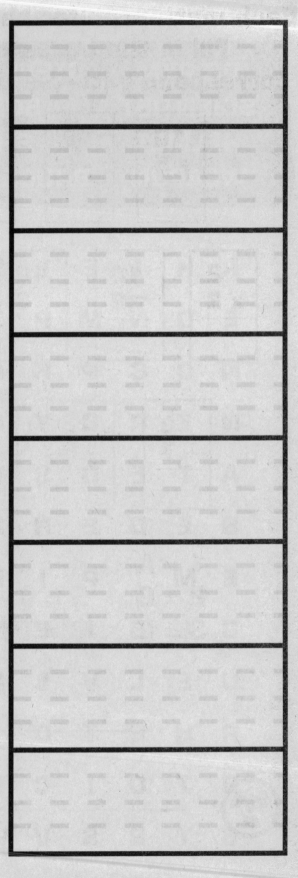

Possible Answers: an, can, ban, bran, fan, Japan, pan, plan, ran, span, tan, than, van

What was the source of Hulk's strength?
Each math problem has a letter-coded answer. Fill in the boxes with the letters that correspond with the correct number answers.

10 ÷ 5	7 - 6	14 ÷ 2	2 + 5	13 - 12

2 x 2	10 - 2	12 ÷ 3	6 + 5	15 - 13	3 x 3

3 + 7	15 ÷ 5	0 + 1	9 - 4	2 x 3

1 = A   4 = E   7 = M   10 = B
2 = G   5 = S   8 = N   11 = R
3 = L   6 = T   9 = Y

___ ___ ___ ___ ___

 ___ ___ ___ ___ ___

___ ___ ___ ___ ___

Answer: Gamma Energy Blast

Dalmatian Press

Which pieces complete the puzzle?

A  **B**  **C**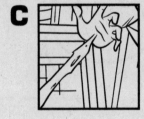

D  **E**

Captain America to the rescue! Finish drawing him.

Can you sort out the picture?
Label each strip according to the correct sequence.

A B C D E F G H

1	2	3	4	5	6	7	8

Answers: F, E, C, G, A, D, H, B